Praise

'In writing *The Limited Edition Leader*, Paula Dunn has developed a wonderful resource for women, regardless of age or status. While it is an ideal resource for teenage girls and their mothers, this book provides valuable insights and practical advice for all women seeking to conquer life with a confident mindset. Paula details instances from her own life and the struggles she experienced in school, with her family, and as a young professional seeking fulfilment and success in her career. She deals with these issues openly and honestly and tracks her pathway to becoming the "leading lady" in her own life. As Paula states: "As parents we want to raise daughters who are the best versions of themselves that they can be." *The Limited Edition Leader* provides a valuable pathway to making this goal a reality, by supporting our daughters to be themselves, and to have the courage and the confidence to conquer life.'

— **Dr Frank Pitt**, former principal,
St Mary Star of the Sea College

'*The Limited Edition Leader*, holds a mirror up to the challenges facing many girls and young women and their families across varied communities. Driven by her own experiences, challenges and triumphs, Paula Dunn's book navigates multiple pathways, through rocky adolescence to parenthood, offering new perspectives. She explores the power of affirmation, resilience and female agency at a time of change that requires young women to demonstrate courage, commitment and solidarity. I commend Paula on her tenacity in confronting the social and emotional paradigms that inhibit our young women from thriving.'

— **Tanya Appleby**, principal,
St Ursula's College, Toowoomba

'Paula's brilliant book is brimming with lightbulb moments. Her wise words about perfectionism and external validation really resonated with me: "Why didn't my career progression, titles and accolades give me a sense of fulfilment?" So many of us forget to celebrate our accomplishments. We simply move on to the next challenge and the exhausting, soul-destroying cycle continues. I'm one of those people who's always been defined by her career. Finding definition in values instead creates new opportunities for growth. These are wise words that I will pass on to my teenage daughter. I also appreciate the narrative about being your own "leading lady", by working on yourself from within. This is important advice for girls and women alike. Overall, what I enjoyed most about this book was its scientific perspective. This is not a "you go, girl!" exhortation. Rather, Paula takes robust scientific research and explains it in layperson's terms, to support the next generation of teenage girls. Highly recommended!'

— **Tracey Spicer**, global keynote speaker/emcee, media and presentation trainer, author and broadcaster

'Paula brings a scientific mind to her own self-reflection. Her explanation of Gen Xers brings clarity to generational differences. Instead of a desire to let herself off the hook, Paula pays grace forward by giving her portion to future women while they are still girls. Paula's vulnerable style matches Brené Brown's sprinkling of four-letter words – it is like a female confessional of honesty. You are not "Dunn" understanding the female crisis until you have read Paula's book.'

— **Michael Grinder**, nonverbal communications expert and National Director of NLP in Education, USA

'In writing this book Paula Dunn has given us a gift. The result is a framework and lessons on how get in touch with the true essence of who you are and to how to live your best life. Through a series of raw and personal revelations, Paula demonstrates that we are amazing just as we are, and we should honour that by being true to ourselves. So many of the lessons resonate with me – I learned them the hard way during my own journey. I wish I'd had access to a book like this, so I could have learned them as a teenager. I especially love the lessons around impostor syndrome, putting self-doubt aside and seeing in yourself what others see in you, taking action and letting your values define you. I highly recommend reading this book and then taking action. Thank you, Paula. You truly are a Limited Edition Leader.'

— **Julie Hyam Elliott**, Williamson Fellow, managing director, board chair and company director

'What can we do to ensure our children grow up to be confident, happy and fulfilled? Paula Dunn leverages her scientific background, extensive research and lived experience to write this excellent guide for high-school students looking to cultivate confidence, courage and self-belief. In *The Limited Edition Leader*, Paula provides teenagers with the personal tools to overcome life's challenges, understand what they truly deserve (not what *others* think they deserve) and build a powerful mindset for personal success. Paula guides young adults to step out of their comfort zone, embrace challenges and find purpose and meaning in their lives.'

— **Jane Jackson**, author of *Navigating Career Crossroads*, LinkedIn Top Voice 2020 and host of *Your Career Podcast*

'If I only had the chance to gift my younger self a few books to help me raise my two daughters, Paula's book would be one of them. In a concise book that does away with the "blalalala" and superfluous, complicated language, Paula provides a guide that every parent should have to nurture their teenage daughters to be confident, resilient and happy. Equipped with her scientific analytical background and drawing on her personal experience, Paula has written a book that is attention-grabbing, easy to read and practical.'

— **Dr Majeda Awawdeh**, founder and managing director, Global Education Academy

PAULA DUNN

BBiomedSc(Hons), MSc(Hons)

THE
LIMITED
EDITION
LEADER

CREATE CONFIDENCE
TO CONQUER LIFE

R^e think

First published in Great Britain in 2021
by Rethink Press (www.rethinkpress.com)

© Copyright Paula Dunn

Cover image © Shutterstock | rudall30

Limited Edition Leader is a registered trademark.

This book is dedicated to all the hard-working Gen X mums out there who were told they were not good enough, brave enough or smart enough to dream big

Contents

Foreword   1

Introduction   5

1 Steps To Creating Confidence   13

   Defining moments   14

   Where focus goes, energy flows   19

   The secret sauce of successful
   people   22

   Life is not about stability   26

   Don't 'fake it till you make it'   29

2 Confidence   31

   The power of ego, emotions and
   external influence   33

   Be the leading lady in your life   35

   The scarcity vs abundance mindset   37

   Control vs chaos   40

3 Limited Edition Leadership   **43**

The Limited-Edition Leadership
methodology   45

Confidence   46

Conscious inclusion   49

Cultivation   51

Congruence   54

Collaboration   56

4 Identity Shapes Destiny   **61**

The influence of parental beliefs   66

Perception is projection   69

How I see myself   70

How I want to be seen   77

How others see me   79

What you believe, you achieve   82

What doesn't kill you makes
you stronger   86

Conclusion   **91**

A goal without a plan is just a wish   93

References   **99**

Further Reading   **105**

Acknowledgements   **111**

The Author   **113**

Contact   113

Foreword

I first met Paula by accident when an article I had written landed in her letterbox due to an incorrect postal address. This fortuitous event brought us together and, as a result, Paula and I learned that we had a great deal in common: that is, the underlying belief in the capacity of girls and women, and the fact that both of us were dedicating our lives to this important cause. For there can be no greater mission in life than positively influencing and shaping the lives of girls and young women.

The Limited Edition Leader brings to the fore the importance of assisting girls in their leadership development to combat issues such as self-doubt and the fear of failure; both of which may arise due to a lack of self-confidence. Paula highlights the importance of mentoring girls and women in this process, thus guiding them towards developing the mindset and skills required to reach their full potential.

Paula emphasises the importance of confidence in this passage towards becoming a Limited Edition Leader, and the ways in which we can assist both ourselves and others to develop capacity in this area. Paula's leadership methodology – consisting of confidence, conscious inclusion, cultivation, congruence and collaboration – provides a framework from which to work. This guiding path highlights the need for girls and women to be self- and socially aware, to foster a growth mindset, to stay true to personal values, and to work with as well as support others.

Of particular importance, Paula addresses the need for girls and women to move out of their comfort zone, to embrace challenge and change and thus shift into a growth mindset where they have identified their purpose through a process of self-acceptance and gratitude. Paula highlights that it is what we see in ourselves, rather than what others see in us, that is the most important realisation we can have. This seemingly simple task is often the greatest challenge for girls and women.

Drawing from her own personal place of adversity, Paula shows us what it is to be a strong woman: a 'leading lady of [her] own destiny' who has learned to accept challenge and grow from the experience. Through her generosity of spirit, Paula shares this experience as well as her expertise in the area of cognitive science, so that we may learn through her and thus facilitate our own development and growth. There is a Limited Edition Leader in all of us, and through Paula's guidance, we can start the journey to this place of acceptance, confidence and success.

As an educator of girls as well as a mother of three daughters, I recognise the importance of Paula's words in this book, and I know that we *all* have a role to play in ensuring that *all* girls are provided with the opportunity to develop their leadership skills and capacity – for who are we to stand in the path of greatness.

Dr Nicole Archard
Principal, Loreto College, Marryatville,
South Australia

Introduction

Have you ever wondered what makes some people successful and others not? I have. For a long time, I looked outside myself, using the lens of comparison to gauge my level of success. I thought my achievements would generate self-confidence and reassurance, and that would make me feel good about myself. But one day, I realised I was doing it all wrong and this lens didn't make me feel good at all. If you're always comparing yourself to others, you'll never measure up. I've learned that self-confidence is generated through self-knowledge, which enables you to understand your fears, overcome them and take control of your destiny. This is what helps you to achieve your version of success, rather than anyone else's, and this is what makes you feel good about yourself.

Research shows that women tend to seek external validation more than men.[1] You know how it goes: get good grades, finish high school, get into the right course at the right university, score a dream job that's aligned to your 'why', roll in the money, marry prince charming, buy a house, have kids and live an 'Instagram life'. Right? Err, can I get a unanimous 'fake news!' Instead, it's more like freak out, stress over exams and worry about the future, jump through that hoop, breathe a sigh of relief – phew. Get into uni, freak out, stress over exams and worry about the future, jump through that hoop, breathe a sigh of relief – phew. Compete for a job, freak out, stress over the interview and worry about the future, jump through that hoop, breathe a sigh of relief... and so it goes on and on, stuck in a never-ending spiral of freak-outs, fuck-ups and faux pas.

We're told that if we are good girls, treat others as we would like to be treated, study hard and work hard, we'll reap the rewards of a great life. Instead, we have careers where we're

---

1   S Hügelschäfer and A Achtizger, 'On confident men and rational women'

unappreciated, bosses who devalue our abilities, and colleagues or clients who degrade us and diminish our self-worth. We become a cog in the wheel of life until one day we run out of steam, lose our shit and find that we have mental health issues. Wonderful.

What's a girl to do? Commonly, we turn to external influences to cope with our anxieties and disappointments about the way our life has turned out. Some of us turn to having the odd glass – or, ahem, bottle – of Dutch courage; others self-medicate, whether prescribed or procured in alternative ways; still others find comfort in food. We all self-soothe in different ways, though each can be a form of self-sabotage.

So, where did we go wrong? What happened to our hopes, dreams and aspirations? Has Generation X got it all wrong? I thought we had it all figured out. We watched our parents be slaves to society, chasing financial security. We saw them lose their job security during the economic crashes of the 1980s and 1990s, with the 'recession we had to have'. We did not want to end up like them. We rejected the notion of working all our lives only to retire with a shitty superannuation payout and, if we were extremely lucky, enjoy the perks of a government pension, with the bonus of $2.00 public transport.

When did we lose control of our lives? The short answer to this question is: the day we lost control of ourselves. We need to take back control and conquer life from within. We lost ourselves by trying to meet society's expectations of us, rather than creating our own. We lost ourselves because we allowed others to determine our destiny. Have you followed the path that society expected from you? And do you feel satisfied with and fulfilled by that path? Are you hoping that your daughter will have the confidence to choose the path that is truly right for her? My aim is to lead young women to find their identity early in life, rather than coming to it much later, like I did. I derive great satisfaction from providing them with what I lacked: a mentor who can see their strengths and what's holding them back from achieving their full potential. A mentor who can guide them to realise their dreams.

Did you know that the number one challenge women and girls face today is self-doubt?[2] It is

2   K Kay and C Shipman, *The Confidence Code*; N Archard, 'Women's participation as leaders in society'

holding us back in a big way. Self-doubt manifests in three common fears:

1. **Fear of self:** This generally arises as feeling like a fraud, feeling as though we don't deserve a seat at the table when we do. This has also been dubbed 'impostor syndrome', an apt name for this common sensation. As a result of this fear, we play small, perhaps we even self-sabotage to prove to ourselves that we are not worthy. This fear can result from persistent negative chatter in our heads, other people's negative opinions of us, and our perception of what others think.

2. **Fear of failure:** This plays out through giving in and giving up, or not trying at all.

3. **Fear of the future:** This makes an appearance as work/life imbalance and results in us compromising across all levels of our lives. We remain stuck in areas of our lives that we know, deep down, if we had the guts to change, we would. Here's a question: If you won a million dollars, what is the first thing you would do to improve your quality of life? Would money give you the courage to

pursue a new venture? Perhaps leave the job you've been complaining about to start your own business? Dump your partner because you're being taken for granted? Start a charity for something you're passionate about?

The bottom line is that we harbour a deep internal belief of 'I'm not enough.' These feelings are often apparent by the tender age of fifteen. I surveyed 100 female Year 10 Australian high-school students and their top fears were: confusion about who they are as a person, feeling stress under pressure and a lack of control over their environment. These directly translate to fear of self, fear of failure and fear of the future. When you're in a room talking with girls about their internal fears, you can't swing a cat. We all have them, as women and as girls. Even the most confident suffer from these fears at one time or another. If you have a friend who says she never feels insecure, she's full of you know what. We've all experienced it, but it's especially common in high achievers or when playing outside your comfort zone.

I lived with these beliefs for most of my life. Being born with a birth defect on my face placed my vulnerability on display for the world to see. It's also what eventually led me to overcoming these limiting ways of seeing the world, putting me on my path to assisting others to overcome their limitations. My background in the cognitive and behavioural sciences, combined with over twenty years of industry experience, including positive psychology, leadership and life coaching, has given me many insights and has led me to develop a methodology for overcoming limitations and enabling peak performance for the girls I work with. My unique programme teaches girls a set of cognitive and behavioural skills, guiding them to better understand themselves and change their behaviours, and giving them knowledge and insights that put them on the fast track to living their best life. This methodology is called the Limited Edition Leader®, and it encompasses the 5Cs: confidence, conscious inclusion, cultivation, congruence and collaboration.

This book contains everything I wish I could have given my younger self, the tools needed to thrive throughout high school and beyond. How to be confident, courageous and live life on your own terms, in your own unique way, with no limits and without feeling you have to people-please. If you (or your daughter) are the type of person who stresses over their future, friendships and relationships; who overthinks and worries about what others think; who procrastinates; who compares themselves to others; who people-pleases, or suffers from perfectionism, then my insights can help you.

I will show you how cultivating confidence, courage and certainty starts from within. We will explore the 5Cs and learn how to implement this methodology in your life. Are you ready to conquer life with a confident mindset?

1

Steps To Creating Confidence

Here's the good news: our brains are pliable. Scientists call this neuroplasticity.[3] Before we understood this neuroplasticity, scientists believed that we couldn't change our way of thinking and behaving. Cognitive science has now proved otherwise, that our brains can be trained and changed. We don't have to stay stuck in beliefs generated by fear; we can create new, empowering beliefs that will serve us better going forward.

Since the emergence of Covid-19, we have learned a lot about pandemics and the real threats to our survival as a species. These

---

3   B Ng, 'The neuroscience of growth mindset and intrinsic motivation'

threats are exacerbated by uncertainty and fear around our health, our jobs and our Australian way of life, which now includes walking around worried about who might give us a virus. Everyone is a potential threat. In addition to all these external fears, we can easily be our own worst enemies when it comes to our advancement.

Fear plays a big role in determining our level of success, and it is often those internal fears: fear of self, fear of failure and fear of the future. If these fears are not controlled, they can totally derail our careers, our relationships and our lives. Learning how to take control of fear and channel it will propel us forward, towards our true north. Taking control of fear requires understanding how it works. The first step is to prepare your mind to take in this new information, so let's pull back those blinders that have been holding you back from being who you were truly meant to be.

Defining moments

'You get what you believe you deserve in life, not what you truly desire.' When I first heard this saying at one of the motivational seminars of Tony Robbins, a professional development guru,[4] it jarred with me. You get what you believe you deserve in life? So, all the bad things that have happened in my life are *my* fault? My initial reaction was, 'Screw you, Tony Robbins!' But then I dug deeper.

I learned that everything comes back to defining moments. A defining moment is something that has an impact on our life, on how we see the world or how we see ourselves. Defining moments don't have to be big to have a strong impact. It all comes down to the meaning you attach to a particular moment. Let me tell you a story to illustrate a defining moment.

There was once a little girl who was born with a birth defect on her face. Before she started school, she didn't think anything of it. Like all little girls, she enjoyed playing with others. When she started school, however, she noticed that she looked different to the other kids. She also noticed that because she looked different, she found it harder to make friends quickly and be liked.

---

4   Team Tony, 'How to get what you deserve'

She was socially excluded by the other girls in her class, and she was teased daily by the boys in the playground. She was called names like 'train tracks' and 'fat lip'. She was called ugly, stupid and was told she wouldn't amount to anything because of the way she looked. She was also physically hurt, kicked in the shins, often going home from school with new bruises or bleeding.

One day, in Grade One, the little girl approached her teacher and told her she was being bullied. The teacher pointed at the door, shouting, 'Go away. Don't tell tattle tales.' The little girl walked away with her head down.

At that *defining moment*, the little girl created a set of internal beliefs:

- Her feelings didn't count.

- She was 'less' than everyone else.

- Her truths were considered lies.

- Those in authority turn a blind eye.

The bottom line: she developed feelings of shame and guilt about who she was. She developed certain behaviours, and in response:

- She allowed people to overstep her boundaries

- She became a perfectionist

- She became a people pleaser

- She desperately wanted to remain invisible

This little girl was in emotional pain, suffering daily from taunts, ridicule and social isolation throughout her primary school years, which were all about survival.

You might have guessed that this little girl was me. I was six years old. Although I didn't know it at the time, this was a defining moment for me. The beliefs I internalised, those one-sided 'truths', became part of me. The meaning I gave to that moment became part of my identity. I wasn't worthy enough. I wasn't good enough to be protected and supported by adults. I believed that if those in authority couldn't help me, how was I going to be able to help myself?

I believed that I had no internal power, and that belief began to define me. I unconsciously gave control to others, creating a helpless, victim mindset. This led to a cycle of feeling helpless and hopeless and, at times, angry and filled with blame and shame. I'd say to myself, 'If I was born normal, I wouldn't be bullied', or 'If I was born normal, I would be liked by others.' I internalised the bullying, believing that it was my fault, that I deserved what I got because I wasn't normal, perfect or pretty.

Others develop a similar victim mindset as a result of their own adverse childhood experiences. Defining moments create internal beliefs, behaviours and actions that can be self-defeating, and we don't even realise we are setting up this internal programming system. These types of defining moments start being programmed into us from the point we are identified by our genitalia. This process of defining us and restraining our identity, putting us into categories or boxes, happens between the ages of nought to seven (the imprint period) and then again between the ages of eight to thirteen (modelling period). Between the ages of fourteen to twenty-one (socialisation period) these programmes become embedded into our psyche and people can often spend the remainder of their lifetime imprisoned within them. The social-isation period is the most dominant growth and development stage, the time when we develop our identity and form beliefs about how we fit into the world around us.[5]

Can you see, then, how defining moments can lead to beliefs that are limiting and self-defeating? Beliefs that we unconsciously enact in our lives because we think that's who we are. The phrase, 'You get what you believe you deserve in life' might make a little more sense now. So, what do we do about this? The first step to creating a thriving and successful life is to examine our internal beliefs and see which concur with who we really are, and which have been programmed into us.

Where focus goes, energy flows

Where focus goes, energy flows. This is a problem. Why? It's a problem because what we believe about ourselves impacts our decisions and what we achieve in life. Remember that what we believe comes from our internal programming, either moving us towards or away from our true desires. You can see this in action by watching an episode of *Married at First Sight.*

---

5   BM Newman and PR Newman, *Theories of Adolescent Development*

You'll see the patterns of behaviours that play out between the couples. They desperately want to find love but continue to sabotage their relationships due to their internal programming. Their programming is leading them away from their desire, because they are blindly following unconscious internal beliefs.

Research has shown that if we reprogram old beliefs and embed new ones that positively support us, we can thrive, flourish and make an impact.[6] Yet how can we control where our focus and energy go so that we can start to reprogram our inner thoughts and feelings?

Science has discovered a part of the brain that controls our attention, arousal, modulation of muscle tone and ability to focus; it's called the reticular activating system (RAS). The RAS is activated through our five senses – sight, sound, taste, touch and smell – and it plays a major role in our survival. It is responsible for our fight and flight responses to external threats, triggering the brain into action or inaction.[7]

---

6   M Stoycheva and P Ruskov, 'Growth mindset development pattern'
7   SS Yeo et al, 'The ascending reticular activating system from pontine reticular formation to the thalamus in the human brain'

Whether or not our RAS is activated is based on our thoughts and feelings about perceived threats. Notice that I didn't say 'threats', but 'perceived threats'. Our perception of threat is influenced by a variety of factors:[8] our personal experiences (including beliefs we've internalised through defining moments), societal and cultural beliefs, religious or spiritual beliefs, and political beliefs.

Most people, though, are unaware of having these beliefs because they are ingrained at a young age and we build upon them over our entire lives. The more often we experience similar events, the more validation a belief can gain. Beliefs become our truths, our normal. But these beliefs or truths may not match reality, and the meaning we create from these beliefs, the significance we give to certain events – such as the significance I gave to the words my teacher spoke to me as a six-year-old – can take us off course or even destroy our lives.

The meanings we attribute and the significance we assign influence our perception of threats, and thus what will activate our RAS. If

---

8   KA Jellinger, 'Funktionelle Pathophysiologie des Bewusst-seins [Functional pathophysiology of consciousness]'

we find going to parties stressful, for example, this will activate our RAS, but if it's something we enjoy, then it won't. If we want to change what activates our RAS, we have to change the meaning we attribute to situations, beliefs and defining moments. By making this change to how we perceive threats, we can take control of where our focus and energy goes.

The secret sauce of successful people

I've spent twenty years modelling and researching the qualities and character traits that successful people have in common. You may be surprised to learn that successful people have a particular attitude that enables them to outperform and outmanoeuvre even the most intelligent people. If you were given the chance to sit in a room with a PhD scholar who chews on data and talks about what makes someone successful, or rub shoulders with Sir Richard Branson, who actually *is* successful, who would you be more interested in meeting? I know who I'd prefer to spend time with, – it would be Richard Branson, no brainer. There's something magical about seeing a real person in action, creating the results you want in your own life. Someone who walks the talk. Successful people do have something in common and it comes back to the 5Cs, which we'll get to soon. In the meantime, let's look at what prevents people from becoming successful.

A large part of the problem is security. The majority of people spend their whole lives ensuring that their need for security is met – in their careers, their relationships and their finances. If you're a Gen Xer like myself, you would have grown up with these beliefs: get a good education, get a stable job, find a partner, settle down, buy a house, push out 2.3 kids, and try to juggle being a mum and career woman.

Sex and the City was my go-to for feeling like I wasn't alone in navigating adult life and relationships, knowing that even Carrie Bradshaw and her successful friends didn't have their shit figured out. I felt like I was part of the group, and it felt good. This was an era where we didn't live on social media or confess our dirtiest secrets online. We wouldn't mark the end of our relationship by updating our Facebook status to 'Single' or 'It's complicated'. But even our choices in TV fed into a quest to feel like we weren't alone; it was all about security, stability and fitting in.

There's nothing wrong with wanting a stable life; the problem occurs when stability breeds a false sense of confidence or complacency. When the need to feel safe and secure in our environment comes to dominate everything else. Only when everything in our lives is perfect will we feel that we're in control and be confident in ourselves. Let me ask you a question, though: when are the circumstances ever completely right? I've been waiting for the 'right time' for a lot of things in my life. One example is planning to have children. This is one of the biggest commitments a person can make. After all, once you have a baby you can't give it back or change your mind. Being a woman who values her career, it's been one of those sticky points for me to determine when was the 'right' time. I spent years and years rationalising that it wasn't yet the right time. My self-talk was that the time would be right 'When we are married', 'After I'm promoted', 'After we buy a house, 'After we've travelled more and enjoyed more life experiences...' and so on and so on.

And do you know what? That right time never came. If I dig deep and am completely honest with you, it wasn't that I needed to tick all those things off my list before making that decision; it was fear of the unknown. How would a baby impact my life? Would it be born healthy or would it have issues? Would I lose my great career and be stereotyped as being unreliable and not serious? Would I still have time for me? Would my body change forever? All these unknowns caused me to stay stuck in a cycle of procrastination and overthinking.

People will complain about everything in their lives but never do anything about it. They have a problem for every solution. Some great examples of excuses people make that limit their lives include:

- I don't have the time
- I don't have the money
- I wasn't born into the right family and don't have connections
- I'm not attractive enough
- I'm not smart enough
- I have a mortgage to pay and family responsibilities

You may think that those are valid points. I agree that they are. Yet these excuses have their origin in fear. Fear of changing the status quo, even if the status quo sucks big time. Remember, humans *love* stability. Our desire for certainty influences everything we think, feel and, ultimately, do. This can cause you to rationalise away all your hopes, dreams and aspirations. If left unchecked, you can lose the essence of who you are and who you were meant to be.

You may be one of the people I'm describing. If you are, the fact that you're reading this book means you're thinking about making some changes, so congratulations! That's the first step in the right direction.

I'll let you in on a little secret. The right time is *when you decide it's the right time.* The difference between a successful person and one who leads a life of quiet desperation[9] is action. They don't let excuses get in the way of their dreams. In the words of Nike: 'Just do it!'

Life is not about stability

If you think life is about stability, you've missed the point. If you can see that security

---

9   'The mass of men lead lives of quiet desperation'
     – HD Thoreau, *Walden*

is an issue of yours, you need to unplug from the matrix. Groupthink, herd mentality and other group biases can mind-fuck you into submission. A great example of this was at the beginning of the coronavirus outbreak, when masses ran to their local supermarket in search of the holy grail: toilet paper. Once some people started doing it, others followed, worrying that if they didn't, they would run out, leading to mass hysteria. The need for security outweighed any semblance of reason.

I was left scratching my head as I watched these events. Irrational behaviour trumps rational thought. I hate to break it to you, but no one gets out of here alive. It's up to you to decide whether you want to let the external environment dictate your sense of certainty, your confidence and clarity, or whether you want to take back control and create the confidence to conquer life your way.

Let's start with clarity. First, you need to understand who you are. Your identity. What makes you, you. Before you even contemplate your why,[10] work out what your strengths are, your weaknesses, your blind

---

10   S Sinek, *Start with Why*

spots. What motivates you, demotivates you? What are your aspirations – however scary – your goals, your values, your beliefs? Become an expert on yourself. You cannot be of use to anyone if you're not of service to yourself, and you can't be useful to yourself if you don't understand your motivations. With the rise of globalisation, the gig economy and artificial intelligence, and now threats to our very existence from pandemics and viruses such as Covid-19, we must flip the switch and develop our certainty from within.

Our parents, and especially our grandparents, lived in a different time, in a society where they had to toe the line and adhere to cultural norms with limited room to be different. Women were forced into the mould of marrying and having children. Men were the breadwinners. They let societal norms – a set of rules, obligations and beliefs – determine their destinies. Life choices were made based on what other people would think, not on what an individual truly wanted out of life. We don't live in that world now. We can and must be proactive. Don't let security blind you to what truly matters to you.

Don't 'fake it till you make it'

Have you ever heard the ridiculous saying, 'Fake it till you make it'? Google it and I'm sure there will be workshops, self-help books and women's networking groups that repeat this blanket statement that is supposed to cure all your insecurities about work, relationships and life. What if I told you that this is complete BS? What would you think? Would you feel liberated? Confused? Who would you believe?

Let's break it down. 'Fake it' implies that you're a fraud or impostor and what you have to offer is not genuine. It's saying that you don't have the talent, ability or skill within you to achieve, so you have to pretend. The 'till you make it' part implies that you haven't made it yet, that you're still waiting for that other shoe to drop, that smell of success, recognition, gaining that grade/mark. Whatever success might look like to you.

When you repeat the phrase 'Fake it till you make it', how does it make you feel now? Furious? Frustrated? Does it reaffirm an internal belief? This was the advice I was given when starting out in my career. A quick-fix mantra that I should be chanting on a daily basis to give me the 'confidence and courage' to take risks and dream big. In reality, though, it just fed my insecurities and the impostor monster even more.

You see, the human brain tricks us into picking up the negative things in our environment. Whether they're real or not, our wiring cannot tell the difference. Research has shown that the majority of our thoughts are negative.[11] When you're telling yourself to 'fake it', your brain believes that you *are* faking it. If this is part of your daily self-confidence boost routine, stop it now. You heard me. *Stop!* If you do want some motivational mantras, I suggest they start with 'I am...'

It's hard enough as it is being a woman, and to imply that we don't deserve a seat at the table until we've 'made it', and until then we should fake it, perpetuates our insecurities, destroys our self-confidence and keeps us from breaking that glass ceiling.

---

11   CS Dweck, *Mindset*; E Selby et al, 'Understanding the relationship between emotional and behavioral dysregulation'

2
Confidence

As women, a lot of our confidence comes from aspects of our external lives. For some of us we focus on our appearance, because society tells us that beauty is sexy, is confidence, is healthy, indicates 'good genes' and creates ample opportunities. For others, myself included, we attach our confidence to our careers. For some, it's who they marry or their children, while for others it's material possessions. You may have a preference for one over another, or your confidence may derive from several of these external factors. Wherever it comes from, the point I am making is that we tend to look outside of ourselves for confidence. Unfortunately, this type of confidence is like eating fast food; it satisfies us for a short time because we're starving, but it does not sustain and nourish us over the long term. This kind of confidence is self-serving and shallow.

What is the problem with this? Why is it self-serving and shallow? As I mentioned earlier, where focus goes, energy flows. If we focus our energy on our appearance to give us confidence, we will always be chasing the next fad. Botox, filler injections, lip flips, breast augmentation, cosmetic tattooing, plastic surgery, the list goes on. We will gain external validation from others' perceptions of whether we are attractive or not.

But the bottom line is:

- Looks will fade
- Careers can be lost
- Marriages can break down
- Children grow up and/or may not become the people we had hoped
- Material possessions can be lost, destroyed or stolen

When we went into lockdown in March 2020, many of us lost what once gave us a sense of confidence. What do we do once we lose our external validation? Many of us feel worthless, because what was propping us up was the fast-food version of confidence. Can you see the importance of developing internal confidence and self-driven leadership?

If I'm telling you that faking it till you make it is wrong, then what? How do we develop the sort of nourishing internal confidence that will sustain us? Instead of looking outside ourselves, we need to look inside to what is valuable to us, rather than what society tells us is valuable. What do *we* value most? What makes *us* feel good about ourselves? Focusing our energy on what truly matters to us will remove our reliance on external validation, and move it to where it should be located, in direct relation to our deepest desires. This type of nourishing confidence, aligned to what matters to us most, will activate the RAS in a positive way. Your RAS will work with you to achieve your dreams instead of working against you, out of fear.

The power of ego, emotions and external influence

Creating confidence is like creating an internal superpower. It's about having the capacity to lead yourself across all aspects of your life, especially during turbulent times, without being led astray by your ego, your emotions or by others.

Let's give confidence some context and talk about superheroes. Who doesn't love a good Marvel comic book or film? This is a good way to discuss confidence with your daughter.

Let's talk about Captain Marvel. Due to a freak accident, she lost her memory. As a result of that moment of vulnerability, she was led astray by someone close to her. Yon-Rogg created a new identity for her, one based around who they wanted her to be. This led to her creating internal assumptions about her limitations and combat capabilities. Yet she felt that something wasn't right, and this came out through recurring dreams. She knew that the dreams were somehow related to her internal misgivings, the feeling that she was living an incongruent life. It wasn't until she started to question the status quo and looked inside herself for answers that she was able to uncover her true identity and unleash her ultimate power. That power came from within. Once she found her truth, she was able to disregard and overpower those who were trying to restrain her, enabling her to get in touch with her power and her ability to save both herself and the world.

Be the leading lady in your life

What does the example of Captain Marvel teach us? It's all about being the leading lady in your own life. How do we achieve the clarity, courage and certainty to be our own leading ladies? We do it by taking back control, and the first step to taking back control is to decide that you want to be that leading lady. Abandon the false sense of security that comes from external validation, from how society says you should look or behave, what grades you should get, what clothes you should wear and who you should sleep with. Find out who you are on the inside and put all your effort into becoming the person that is aligned with your values, your desires, your priorities.

Make the decision that you want to be you. This is important because making this decision recognises *our control over our choices*. Our choices impact everything we do and don't do: the career choices we make, our friendships and the people we hang around, the life partners we choose, how we prioritise our time looking after our health and well-being, how we choose to spend and invest our money and, ultimately, how we influence and impact our children.

Who are your role models? Do you have anyone that inspires you? Research those who inspire you, famous or not. Write down the reasons why you admire ten people; think about their qualities and look for common traits. What jumps out at you? Carl Jung, the godfather of modern humanistic psychology, said that it is impossible for us to see external to us what is not already present within us.[12] What does this mean? It means that what you see in those you admire is already present in you in some way. You don't need to become more like them, you just need to recognise what it is you admire about them that is already within you.

Whether you are aware of it or not, you are also a role model. Not just for your children, if you have them, but for everyone with whom you interact. If you have daughters, how they expect be treated is influenced by the example you set of what you tolerate in your own

---

12   A Hopwood, 'Jung's model of the psyche'

relationships. If you have sons, you are their role model for how they should treat the women in their lives. You might also serve as a role model for the friends of your children and even for your own friends. Once you've embraced the role of leading lady in your own life, you will become an even better role model for those around you.

The scarcity vs abundance mindset

Research shows that intelligence and a high IQ don't equate to long-term success in life.[13] Many people who have failed at school have managed to build multimillion-dollar companies from nothing. Why do some of us feel like victims while others feel like victors? It has a lot to do with how we see ourselves.

Let me break it down for you. When you think of the word 'victim', what springs to mind? Perhaps it's something along the lines of a person who had an unfortunate accident that was outside of their control. Or someone who needs to be rescued, because they can't help themselves. What about a 'victor'? This

---

13 N Archard, 'Adolescent girls and leadership'

might sound like someone who is a winner. Someone who is self-driven, in control of their circumstances and knows exactly what to do to win.

Why is it important to understand these two different mindsets? It's important because you need to work out which is closer to your mindset right now. Do you feel like a victim or a victor? When things go wrong or you fail, do you feel that the situation is out of your control? Do you feel that bad things always happen to you and you just have to accept that? Or, do you feel more like a victor, that even if and when you fail you can always work out a plan B and come back from it? Do you know in your heart that even if today sucks, tomorrow will be better? Are you confident that you'll get to where you need to be in the end, even if it takes longer or looks different to how you imagined? Have a think about it for a moment. Which one sounds like you? Be honest.

Having a victim mindset sets you up for believing that everything you want is in short supply and hard to come by. In this way, a victim mindset is also a scarcity mindset, setting you up for failure before you've even begun. You focus on what you have to lose rather than what you have to gain. You start to behave like an animal under threat, feeling as if everyone is in competition with you. You compare yourself to others and notice what you don't have in your life. You envy those who have what you want, but you won't take the risk of trying to get this for yourself, because you don't want to fail. You stay stuck in victim mode, hoping that someone will come and save you from your tragic existence. Then, if that person lets you down, you add them to your persecutor list, reaffirming that everyone is out to get you. If you suffer, so does everyone around you. Misery loves company, right?

By contrast, having a victor mindset sets you up for believing that everything you want is in abundance. You love to collaborate with people and help others, because there's plenty of food on the table. You treat failure as a lesson learned rather than a personal attack on your character. You can handle crises with ease, rather than making them a drama. You go out and get what you want, knowing it's out there in abundance for those willing to risk their security and try.

Make a decision, as the leading lady in your life, that you're going to take advantage of your brain's neuroplasticity and reframe your thinking. Make sure you have a victor mindset.

Control vs chaos

Being so connected and globalised has made it easier to acquire knowledge and services, but it's also created an imbalance. Technology and advancement were supposed to make our lives easier, but in some ways they've made things more complicated. The distraction created by constant connection has led to a sense of chaos and confusion. Through social media we are bombarded with what we perceive as successes, as no one posts about their failures. This leads to higher expectations of ourselves and a desire for the kind of success that can be proven via social media. Consequently, we accentuate only the 'successful' parts of our lives, rather than our whole, authentic, flawed selves.

As adults in a modern, globalised world, we are not only competing locally for jobs, we're competing across different countries, often losing out to cheaper options. The ideal of working hard and reaping the rewards no longer holds the same weight, which creates a paradox: an abundance of resources leads to a mindset of scarcity.

We can't control the macro-economic powers around us, but we can control how we react and respond to our external environment. We can decide how much of our time we give to the distractions of social media. We can reduce the feeling of chaos and the imbalance created through this endless parade of perceived success and we can look within ourselves to create an internal locus of control.

3
Limited Edition Leadership

One in seven students and one in four adults suffer from mental health issues, such as stress, anxiety and depression.[14] We live in a society where it's difficult to keep pace with current innovations. Our education system is struggling to stay relevant, despite its efforts. It's now up to the individual to be accountable for their personal development and relevance in tomorrow's world. As a parent, why allow your daughter to become a statistic, when you can give her the tools to thrive?

I don't need to tell you how important this is, because you've experienced the world's

---

14 Australian Institute of Health and Welfare, *Mental Health Services in Australia*

challenges after high school for yourself. The struggle you had finding your first job, proving your self-worth over and over to get that promotion or piddling pay rise, delivering high quality work so your boss could look good. What about the way you've sacrificed who you are to make others happy? For every compromise you've made for others, you've compromised your identity. Perhaps you're still trying to re-establish your 'why'.

I created the Limited Edition Leader methodology to directly address the five ailments faced by women in the workplace, things that can undermine their confidence and prevent them from achieving success:[15]

1. Self-doubt (addressed through **confidence**)

2. Dealing with unconscious bias (addressed through **conscious inclusion**)

3. Lack of opportunity for promotion (addressed through **cultivation**)

4. Conflicting roles, eg between career and motherhood (addressed through **congruence**)

---

15   E Isaacs, 'Women and leadership report'

5. Lack of support from other women (addressed through **collaboration**)

The Limited-Edition Leadership methodology

Have you noticed that everyone who seems to get what they want in life has a particular air about them? It's confidence. Confidence is the feeling of knowing who you are, regardless of what is going on around you. Confidence is the secret ingredient to success.

If you don't have confidence, you end up like everyone else, fighting for a seat at the table. The glass ceiling is tough to crack because only a certain type of person, with a particular kind of attitude, gets the opportunity to break through it. The rest of us just watch from the other side of the glass, in envy or awe.

Yet it's not that hard to become confident, nor does it take years to achieve. You don't need to accumulate degrees and qualifications to feel more confident. There are just five things you need to conquer life.

The Limited Edition Leader Methodology

Confidence

The first thing to understand is that self-awareness amplifies self-management and confidence. Self-awareness is the most powerful tool you can have in your tool belt. Knowing what is going on inside gives you an edge over most people. It helps you to recognise when your emotions are beginning to overwhelm your thoughts. This is important because when our emotional reactions become over-whelming, inappropriate or disproportionate it can destroy our relationships, both personal and professional.[16]

Inappropriate emotional reactions can happen in one of three ways:

1. We feel and show the right emotion, but at the wrong intensity. An example of this would be a situation where some worry is justified, but we overreact and become terrified.

2. We feel the appropriate emotion, but we show it the wrong way. An example of this would be a situation where anger is justified, but our response (for example, giving the silent treatment) is counterproductive.

3. We feel the wrong emotion altogether. An example of this would be if we are in a toxic relationship and instead of calling out your partner and telling them that it is not acceptable to treat us that way, we keep making excuses for their mistreatment of us. Instead of feeling

---

16   P Eckman, *Emotions Revealed*

justifiably angry, we feel that there must be something wrong with us.

Self-awareness helps us to develop appropriate emotional responses, because it enables us to identify our triggers and control how we respond to them. For example, we might recognise that we're always on edge when we have PMT. If we know this, we have the potential to do something about it, rather than behave reactively and then regretting our angry outburst later.

Self-awareness helps us to develop confidence, as we know what triggers an emotional reaction. It helps us make better choices, including decisions that lower our risk of inappropriate emotional reactions. Understanding who we are and who we want to be gives us confidence. It assists us to overcome the self-doubt that can stop us from reaching our full potential. Having a deeper understanding our beliefs, biases (including unconscious biases) and behaviours gives us confidence in who we are. It gives us the strength to make our own decisions, regardless of what others think, and to act on them. Aligning our values to our goals gives us the humility to overcome setbacks, enabling us to develop resilience and the will to persevere. All these factors feed confidence.

Conscious inclusion

As well as self-awareness, we need to develop social awareness. There's a lot of talk about diversity and inclusion in society, but how can we embrace everyone's uniqueness if we are not 100% clear on our own identity?

Conscious inclusion is only effective if we recognise our biases and beliefs. We all have biases, determined by our belief system. These judgements are part of being human, short-cuts that help us to quickly assess our environment for perceived or real threats. They tend to be elevated in those who have experienced trauma or negative experiences. Our bodies remember the pain of the past, creating an increased need to protect ourselves from repetition of that hurt.

Have you ever been to the optometrist for your yearly eye exam, convinced that there's nothing wrong with your eyesight, only for the optometrist to tell you your prescription has changed? You walk out with a new pair of lenses. Suddenly, you see the world in sharper focus, though you hadn't realised that your vision had been impaired. You had adjusted to suboptimal eyesight without realising it. In a similar way, we each see the world through biased lenses, even though we don't necessarily know it.

Our biases can be a catalyst for emotional triggers, so it's important to learn to recognise how they are created. We form biases in three ways: through *deletion*, *distortion* or *generalisation* of the information we receive. Deletion occurs when we focus only on certain bits of information and ignore the rest. People (often) see only what they want to see. Distortion happens when we interpret information based on our beliefs, or on what we've read, seen or heard. Because we don't have access to unlimited information, we create assumptions based on the limited information that we have, which may not be complete or accurate. Generalisation occurs when we create an overall assumption, assessment or judgement about something or someone, without seeking all the facts. This is where stereotypes come into play.

Conscious inclusion is all about developing the emotional intelligence to understand another person's perspective, including their biases – the way they delete, distort and generalise their world. It's important to recognise where they are coming from, even if we do not agree with them. We are part of a social system and we have to be aware of others – what is happening for them, their needs and their wants, an awareness of their emotions. We can also appreciate their difference and potentially learn something new about ourselves too. We should not simply tolerate others but embrace them as equals.

Becoming open-minded and able to embrace diversity, with a greater awareness of everyone's biases, including our own, will enable us to create confidence within ourselves. We will have an understanding of and confidence in our identity and understand more clearly how others' identities are formed.

Cultivation

With a growth mindset, we learn to be flexible, agile and open to new ways of thinking and being. My father had a fixed mindset. He saw everything as black and white, right or wrong, good and bad; there was no grey area. Everything and everyone needed to be figured out and labelled as either right/ good or wrong/bad. He lived a rigid and unforgiving life and always saw the glass as half empty. He generalised his life as one big disappointment and believed that everything bad that had happened to him was the fault of others. He had distorted views about life, because of his past experiences, and passed these views on to his children. He clung onto the past like a dog with a bone, repeating the same old patterns while expecting a different outcome.

Unfortunately, although I discovered a new way of thinking, I could not save him from himself and help him live a purposeful and happy life. He was too set in his ways. The irony was that he wanted a happy and meaningful life, but he was unable to get out of his own way and achieve it.

Some of the ways that having a fixed mindset can derail your success are:

- Seeing life as one size fits all – having a black-and-white mentality

- Being stuck in the past – thinking that because something has always been done a certain way, that's just the way it is

- Avoiding challenges and difficult situations

- A tendency to be critical and give negative feedback

- Feeling threatened by the success of others

With a growth mindset, on the other hand, you will:

- See the shades of grey in situations, accept that other people see the world in a different way

- Recognise that two people with conflicting ideas can both be right when you consider their perspectives

- Be prepared to learn about new ways of seeing the world, to give up old beliefs when you recognise they aren't helping you and to adopt better ways of being

- Embrace challenges as opportunities for learning and growth, even if you make mistakes

- Accept others and be unthreatened by difference or by others' success

Cultivating a growth mindset enables us to stay true to ourselves while conquering life with confidence.[17] A growth mindset enables flexibility, which is key to achieving our life goals. They may not happen in time frame we'd like, but that doesn't mean we're failing or that our efforts are futile. Not settling for second best takes time and patience. I usually tell my clients that, if they're finding their journey hard, then they're on the right track. There's a misconception that if something is easy then it must be right for you; in reality, pursuing any goal takes effort.

It's important to be clear about your identity before you get to work, as this is what will intrinsically motivate you to continue when others give up. When you face a setback, you will be more likely to see what you can learn from it to improve and continue on your path. If your motivation is generated by someone else's expectations (such as following your parents' dreams) you are more likely to give up when faced with a setback.

Congruence

It's important to stay true to your values and higher purpose, to 'walk the talk'. Life can be

---

17   B Ng, 'The neuroscience of growth mindset and intrinsic motivation'

difficult and sometimes we are roped into situations or environments that are outside our control, whether in a workplace environment or in our personal life. Don't sell your soul for second best. Getting what you want takes time, effort and resources.

Congruence is one of the most vital steps to building your character. Do you say one thing and do another? Doing what you say you'll do demonstrates integrity, strong values and trustworthiness. You only have to look at the political landscape and observe how different leaders (not naming any names) have guided their countries through the pandemic to recognise the integrity (or not) of a leader.

If you're congruent, you will be outwardly focused on helping others rather than keeping your focus internally on helping yourself. Creating a congruent life influences the type of career you'll move into, the type of friendships you'll form and maintain and the type of partner you'll be drawn to. Think of congruence as a mirror: what's facing out at you should be the same as what's facing in.

How do you know whether you're living a congruent life? There's a simple test. Ask yourself:

Do I feel inner peace? Answer yes or no, without thinking too much about it – you're looking for a feeling more than a thought. If you instinctively answered yes, then congratulations, you're already there. If you answered no, then I have another question: What is the first thing you think about when you wake up in the morning and the last thing you think about as you're lying in bed at night? This will give you an inkling as to what is causing the incongruence in your life. Use this insight to make the necessary changes. Do what you say and stay in line with your values as much as you can.

Collaboration

Think about who you need on your team to help you. Women have a tendency not to help each other out, to compete rather than collaborate, due to the scarcity mindset we discussed earlier.[18] This is exacerbated by the difficulties women face trying to make it in a man's world. It's through collaboration, rather than competition, that we thrive.[19] One

---

18 T Vaillancourt, 'Do human females use indirect aggression as an intrasexual competition strategy?'

19 N Archard, 'Adolescent girls and leadership'

of the mistakes I made when I was growing up was thinking I had to figure everything out on my own. If I had help, I believed it showed that I was weak and stupid and couldn't handle it. Yet if you read about successful people, you soon learn that they all had mentors and advisers or surrounded themselves with people who were where they wanted to be, people who provided a source of information and inspiration.

Where did my belief that I had to be self-reliant and do everything on my own come from? It originated in previous generations of my family, who passed on their beliefs to me. They believed that getting help was a sign of a weak character, indicating you didn't have the courage or confidence to make it on your own. Think back to stories you've heard from or about your grandparents. Did they express similar beliefs? Have they ever said things like, 'I did everything on my own, no one gave me a handout' or 'If I wanted to make money, I worked hard for it'? Once I learned the importance of getting other people on board to help me achieve my goals, my personal growth fast-tracked.

It's a similar story in the workplace, and in society in general. We all live in hierarchies and have our place in the world. Hierarchies were born out of patriarchy, a fight for the alpha dog position. As younger generations are entering the workplace, however, hierarchical leadership is no longer considered helpful; instead, collaborative or shared leadership is one of the fastest growing organisational trends to hit modern workplaces.

The great news for Generation Xers is that most of us are starting to experience this new collaborative culture at work. Some of us may be CEOs of our own businesses or leaders in organisations, implementing this approach. Either way, we have the opportunity to steer the ship into unchartered waters through collaboration with our younger aspirational colleagues and, of course, shine a guiding light for our daughters.

Collaboration is all about sharing the load, not having to go it alone; about making decisions as a team and getting input and ideas from each other, so we can make improvements for all.

Those are the five elements of the Limited Edition Leader method. There's no point trying to skip over any of the five steps in the hope that it will fast-track your success. You can try to just be confident, but your confidence will likely show up as arrogance or insecurity. Then you'll be just like everyone else trying to fake it till they make it, which tends to translate as behaving badly and not living your best life. How will you know if you're doing this? You'll find that you:

- Are argumentative, dominating conversations, appearing egocentric and insecure

- Blame others for your problems, stuck in a victim mindset and cycle of negative thinking

- Are oblivious to other people's feelings and are judgemental and critical of others

- Have poor coping skills, overthinking things and worrying about what others think

- Have emotional outbursts, driven by jealousy and learned helplessness

It doesn't sound good, does it? This is why you must follow these five steps if you want to gain the confidence, courage and certainty you need to be your best self. When you reach this state, you will:

- Be collaborative, inspiring others and flourishing together

- Take responsibility for your own actions, both your successes and your mistakes, and learning where you can

- Care for others, supporting them when they fail or lose sight of their dreams

- Have excellent coping skills, making decisions based on your values and goals

- Be emotionally secure, using self-knowledge to understand your sensitivities

4

Identity Shapes Destiny

Understanding our identity is important, as it significantly impacts the way we live, the choices we make and the directions we take. As previously mentioned, our identity is influenced by our beliefs and biases and, in turn, influences our behaviour. Unfortunately, our brains are hardwired to focus on the negative.[20] This is called negativity bias. It means we are always subconsciously on guard, seeking to protect ourselves from those who would harm us. This is especially true if you've had adverse childhood experiences and are continuing to use the past as a guide for your decision-making.

---

20 L Müller-Pinzler et al, 'Negativity-bias in forming beliefs about own abilities'

We each have a comfort zone, and our negativity bias (based on our fears) is like an electric fence around this zone. We feel safe and in control of our surroundings when we're inside it; within these boundaries, we quite confidently know who we are. Our comfort zone is evident in our daily routines, in those matters we don't need to think about or stress over. The size of our comfort zone is dependent on our level of fear and whether we allow our fear to paralyse us and prevent us from taking the next step forward. Three kinds of fear can paralyse us:

1. Fear related to our beliefs – what we believe about ourselves

2. Fear related to our biases – the conscious and unconscious shortcuts we use

3. Fear related to our behaviours – what we choose to do about our beliefs and biases

Our comfort zones will be challenged or compromised by any of these three areas of fear. The fear could arise due to a new situation, or one where we can't control or anticipate the outcome. It could be as small as being scared of looking like an idiot if we stuff up or say the wrong thing during class, or it could be related to something much more serious, such as ongoing bullying or abuse. What we do when our comfort zone is challenged tells us whether or not we're paralysed by fear. If we face challenges head on, secure in our identity (knowing our values and goals), then we won't be paralysed by fear.

Yet most people push against fear and hold on to their comfort zone. This is a completely normal human response. We want to protect ourselves (and our children) from danger. Although this is natural, will doing it repeatedly make us happy? It may seem a successful strategy in the short term, but the long-term consequence is a reluctance to try again, or to take the risk if placed in a similar situation. This could have significant long-term impact, such as feeling dissatisfied, or passing limiting beliefs on to your children, stifling their growth and development. Our comfort zone can become a cage, where our identity is based only on what makes us feel secure, limiting our opportunities for growth. We define ourselves in restrictive ways, such as, 'I'm unattractive,' 'I'm not sporty,' 'I'm not academic.' This limits us, eating away at our life, destroying our career, our relationships and our health.

Yet if we push past our comfort zone and face our fear, the magic starts to happen. The difference between average people and those who succeed in life is the willingness to enter and sit within the fear zone until they've pushed past the boundary of fear and into the learning and growth zone. In this zone, we have greater scope to enlarge our sense of identity, because we haven't boxed ourselves in.

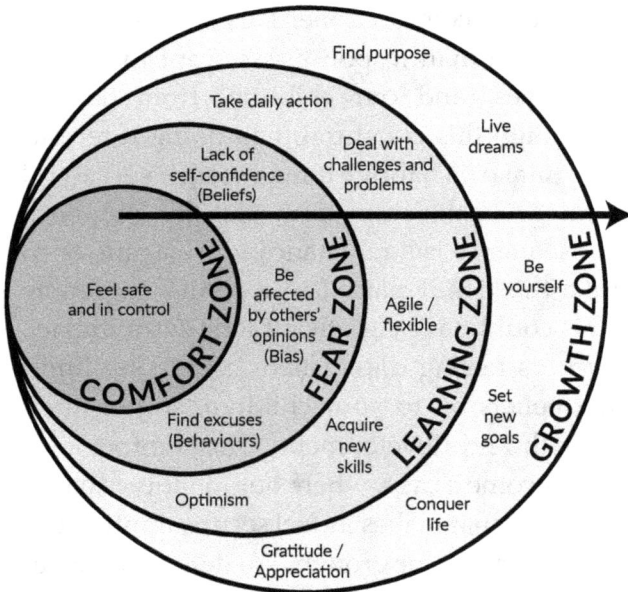

Breaking into the learning and growth zones

I was born with a bilateral cleft lip and palate (deformity of the lip). My parents were fearful about my future and whether I would fit in to society. This fear was based on their own experiences. They had found immigrating to a new country hard, because they couldn't speak the language and had a different culture – despite being born 'normal'. My parents meant well, but sometimes they were just too close to my problems and they had created their own biases about my capabilities.

My parents tried to keep me inside their comfort zone, because they wanted to keep me safe. Their comfort zone became mine, although mine also included isolating myself from others so that I wouldn't be subjected to bullying. My fear zone included a fear of going to school (due to bullying), a fear of social situations (due to being excluded) and fear about my future (due to my parents' fears). Then I learned techniques to control my fear through neurolinguistic programming and realised that it was my values that defined me, not my career. This led me to challenge my fear zone and move into the learning and growth zones.

Now I am in control of my own life and I don't allow others to label me. I launched my business because I wish I'd had access to this information when I was younger so that I could have implemented it sooner.

The influence of parental beliefs

My parents emigrated from Europe to Australia during the 1950s, not long after World War II. It was a time of scarcity; nations had been destroyed, morale was low and people were seeking new opportunities where they could thrive.

My father chose Australia, seeing it as a land of opportunity. He believed there was an abundance of work here and he wanted to create a better life for himself, my mother and his future children. When I think about what it would have been like to leave the place you've grown up, to take the risk of travelling to the other side of the world on a ship... That's ballsy.

Dad was the first in my family to come to Australia, in 1956. He found work, bought a block of land and built a one-room house, before my mother and sister arrived in 1958. Dad used to say how hard it was being a 'New Australian', as nothing was given to you. There were no government subsidies, as there are today; everything had to be worked hard for. Dad never said no to a job, even if it meant travelling long distances to do crappy work for minimal pay.

In those days, New Australians were given laborious menial jobs while the British and Australians had managerial positions. These days, you see a similar dynamic, with many migrants driving Uber cars and delivering Uber Eats, taking what work they can to earn an extra dollar.

Dad learned the language and did his best to fit in to the culture. He learned to speak English by reading the paper. It took him six months of scrounging and saving every penny to buy a plot of land in Wollongong. He built our one-room house with his own hands, when he could. As a New Australian, he wasn't even permitted a bank loan. So many doors were closed to him, yet he thrived financially, due to his staunch work ethic. However, as I've mentioned, many of his beliefs didn't serve him well in the end, and most of them were unhelpful to me; I've had to learn new beliefs so that I can thrive.

How can you push against what's been programmed into you by your parents? I'm sure you have heard stories from your parents and grandparents about what life was like when they were growing up; some will recall happy times, others less happy. I'm not telling you to dismiss your past or resent your family for the lessons they've passed on from their experiences. I am suggesting you analyse your programming, embrace what works for you and recognise what's holding you back. What beliefs will help you to reach your fullest potential, to be your best self?

Think about the stories you've been told and any family sayings. Mine, from my dad, were 'Money doesn't grow on trees' and 'Life wasn't meant to be easy'. Both statements are true and helped my dad in his own life, but they weren't helpful for me and so I let them go. I replaced them with a new set of beliefs that were right for me, beliefs that helped me to pursue the life I wanted to lead. These included, 'Money *does* grow on trees', by which I mean that money is around me in abundance, I just have to go out and get it. Another one is 'No limitations', because I don't want anything to stop me from achieving my goals. What beliefs will help you achieve yours?

Perception is projection

How we see the world greatly impacts how we see ourselves within it. What we perceive within us is what we project around us, feeding into our identity. If we don't have a strong identity, if we don't have self-knowledge and clear goals, it is easy for fear to take over. Why is this? Fear is in our DNA, it's what has helped the human race to survive. Perceived threats, such as the fear we feel preparing for an exam, affect our bodies in the same way as real threats. You know you're not going to die, that there is no risk of physical harm to you, but your body responds in the same way it would if you were facing a lion wanting to eat you for his dinner.

The way we perceive threats is influenced by three things:

1. The way we see ourselves

2. The way we want to be seen

3. The way others see us

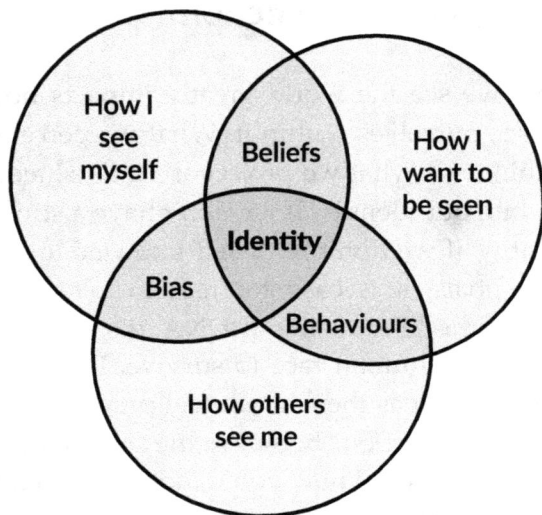

Intersecting identities

How I see myself

I grew up with the belief that I wasn't good enough. I saw myself as less than everyone else and everywhere I looked I saw proof of this. When adults and peers tell you the same thing, over and over, it must be true, right? Yet I also felt an internal conflict. People were saying I wasn't good enough and, on one hand, I believed them, but on the other I was determined not to let their truth become my life sentence. Before I started school, I had seen myself differently: I'd had confidence, courage and self-acceptance. I thought that going to university and getting degrees would repair my self-belief, lead to respect and make me unbullyable. I couldn't wave a magic wand, so I focused on making education my saviour. Yet even after acquiring multiple qualifications, I still felt like that deformed and helpless little girl. Nothing had changed.

What did I do to finally change my self-belief? I started thinking. Why weren't the degrees enough to make me feel whole? Why didn't my career progression, titles and accolades give me a sense of fulfilment? I realised they were all forms of external validation. I thought I needed them to feel worthy, but by the time I reached each goal it felt like nothing. I didn't sit in awe and celebrate my accomplishment; I simply turned my focus to the next thing that was going to make me feel happy and whole. And so the cycle continued.

One day, I took stock. I looked at where I was and where I wanted to be and saw that there was a large gap, but it wasn't a gap based on achievement. I realised that my mindset was not enabling me to create the life I wanted for myself. I had a revelation: 'If I want to change my outside world, I need to change my inside world.' But how the hell was I supposed to do that? Have a lobotomy?

The good news was that I didn't need to go to that extreme, but I did need someone on my team to help. Up until this point I had been asking questions like, 'Why is this happening to me?' and 'Why am I not lucky enough to get want I want?' After my revelation, I began asking new questions: 'Why not me?', which led me to, 'Who do I need on my team to help me create the life I want?'

Being a scientist, I researched my options. I began with the path most travelled, spending thousands of dollars talking to counsellors and psychologists. For a time, it was great; I was able to seek solace from my counsellor and had space to ruminate over the past with my psychologist. I mean, don't we women like to try and make sense of the world around us?

I came out of the sessions feeling as though a weight had been lifted from my shoulders (and from my purse, too). Briefly, I felt heard and validated. I was able to complain about everything that had gone wrong in my life, who had wronged me and why it was everyone's fault but mine. I was a victim of circumstance; it was never me. I was not the common denominator.

Yet, after a while, it felt like I was going round and round in circles, rehashing the same shit. I was getting tired and frustrated. Sometimes I'd come out of sessions scratching my head thinking, 'I spent an hour in there pouring out my heart, yet I'm walking away feeling the same as when I went in.' Don't get me wrong, it was great to receive compassion and talk about the past, but it didn't help me to create a new mindset, new solutions or ways of thinking and feeling about things. It did help me to survive the daily grind, but that was all I was doing, surviving.

Next, I enrolled in various soft skills courses, including leadership, communication, influencing and emotional intelligence. I thought they would complement my technical and scientific skills and be helpful for the future. I was doing it for my career, but also to better understand myself. They helped much more than therapy, because they gave me the background to understand deeper concepts and theories about why we do the things we do.

I drew on my academic prowess to become an expert in human emotions, behavioural styles, communication styles, emotional intelligence, managing difficult people (including psychopaths), positive psychology, coaching psychology, project management, entrepreneurship and leadership. I realised that I loved learning. I loved it because I was on a personal quest to conquer life, but it wasn't enough, something was still missing.

Then I ventured on a path less travelled: life coaching. Once again, my motivation was two-fold: first, it would be good for my career; second, it would facilitate personal growth. Through coaching, I was able to combine all my experience and expertise into applicable and actionable practical techniques that, finally, created the long-lasting change I had been seeking.

I started by working on my beliefs. What were my truths? What did I believe? I realised that my values were misaligned and needed to be reclassified and reprioritised. One of the things they don't tell you when you sign up to study life coaching is that you are your first client. You don't just sit in a class and learn theories and concepts by rote, you put them into action.

You are the guinea pig. For someone with an analytical background, it was challenging, but the benefit of being a scientist is the urge to question everything. I also wanted to experience the techniques and strategies I would be using so that I would be convinced that they worked.

The methodologies I learned as a life coach challenged my thinking and helped me break through the thought patterns that had led to unhelpful behaviours. The lights of my life came on. The awesome thing about it was that I already had everything I needed within me, ready to pull out and use. I didn't need to be 'fixed'. I realised that in fact I *was* the common denominator. I used to blame others and circumstances for why I had drawn the short straw. Now I was blaming myself, but not in a bad way, in a way that meant I could take charge of my life and create the one I wanted, moving forward. I changed how I saw myself. Unless you've tried it, you don't realise the power you have when you decide to own your shit and go on a personal mission to conquer life.

The experience was confronting, as I had to face all my fears head on, but it was also life changing. I resigned from my job and started my own business to help others. I thought, 'All this should have been taught to me when I was a teenager, not at forty.' If I could go back to my younger self, I would tell her that everyone has their own perceptions about life, their own limitations, which come directly from their beliefs and experiences. Yet beliefs, and even past experience, are only one side of the story. You think they define you, when they might not necessarily even apply to you.

Another piece of advice I'd give my younger self is that if something is hard, this means you're growing. You're pushing yourself out of your comfort zone to become a better version of yourself. Many of us have a tendency to give up or give in, because we don't believe in ourselves. Yet making a decision to be your own leading lady is about making a decision to work on yourself from within to make lifelong transformations on the outside. Self-improvement is hard work, all great things are, but it will be worth it in the end. You'll see.

Reflect on yourself. Who are you? And who are you not? Answering these two questions will tell you how you see yourself. As you can see from my journey, I changed my limited perceptions of who I thought I was and became the person I wanted to be. You can do this too, using the Limited Edition Leadership methodology to break through your narrow sense of self.

How I want to be seen

How do you want to be seen? And does this reflect who you really are as a person? How you see yourself is often based on societal perceptions of who you should be, rather than who you truly are. For example, if you want to be seen as cool and popular at school, you might think this equates to drinking alcohol and having sex. This might not be what you want to do, but you do it anyway, because it aligns with your desire for others to see you as cool. This will lead to a sense of incongruence between who you are inside and who you pretend to be in order to be accepted by society.

When I was at primary school, I wanted to be seen as normal; I wanted to be liked and loved, like everyone else. I didn't want to be seen as abnormal, ugly, stupid and sickly. The funny thing was, before I started school, I hadn't seen myself as any of these things. I loved playing with my toys, putting on dance shows and pretending I was on *Young Talent Time*. I didn't have any fears or hang-ups about who I was and what I could achieve. I had a positive sense of my identity, and congruence between who I was and the external world.

When I started school, I started noticing that I was different. The 'pretty' girls were the teachers' pets, they were chosen for everything – reading passages at mass, the main parts in plays, prefects and school captains – and they never seemed to do anything wrong; they were perfect. I used to spend hours looking at these seemingly perfect girls and then going home and studying all my 'imperfections' in the mirror. If there was something I could have done to change my looks, I would have done anything, even if it went against my true identity, just to fit in.

Part of my process of building resilience and enduring the difficult periods of my life was reading stories about the struggles of others, especially those who were physically different but who ultimately triumphed. My search for inspiring role models drove me to overcome the pain in my life and gave me hope, helping me to look to the future. When the present was too painful – because I couldn't change the way I looked or influence other people – I would imagine myself grown up, when all my surgeries were over. My mother had often told me the story of the ugly duckling and I would imagine myself as that beautiful swan, having a perfect life with the same opportunities as everyone else. This gave me something to aspire to. Once I grew up, the future didn't look quite as I'd imagined it, but I used my growth mindset to shape my identity, with congruence, to become the person I'd always wanted to be.

How others see me

Research has shown that social situations impact how we modify our behaviour based on how others see us.[21] Growing up, I was told that I was stupid and ugly, that I wouldn't amount to anything in life and would most likely die young. This was the feedback I received from my primary school teachers, the medical profession and my peers.

---

21   J Steinmetz et al, 'Being observed magnifies action';
     L Müller-Pinzler et al, 'Neural pathways of embarrassment
     and their modulation by social anxiety'

I unconsciously confirmed other people's expectations of me, playing the role I thought was mine. I never challenged other people's judgements, just went along with them. That meant accepting being put on the bench as a reject – the real meaning of a 'reserve' – in netball. It meant accepting that I was a 'slow learner', because I'd been put in the remedial learning class. My parents participated in confirming others' expectations of me. I was in and out of hospital for operations and illnesses relating to my birth defect, so I was classified as sickly and weak. My parents reinforced this, by being overprotective and not allowing me to join in school activities, with my mum yelling at me to put on a jumper each time I sneezed.

The situation would have been different if my parents, or teachers, had been aware of conscious inclusion. Instead, their unconscious biases led them to turn a blind eye to my real needs, as well as my strengths. If my teacher had been consciously aware of the bullying that was going on in class, she might have seen that it wasn't my intelligence that was lacking.[22] In reality, my anxiety was the underlying cause of my learning difficulties.

---

22   L De Luca, 'The teacher's role in preventing bullying'

I reached a turning point when I started high school. I was patiently waiting to see if I would be accepted, as my bullies at primary school had said, 'You won't get in; you're too stupid.' I remember receiving my acceptance letter; they'd been proven wrong. The school motto, written on our diary, was, 'I am born for higher things.' For me, getting into that school meant exactly that: I had been born for higher things. They had accepted me. Contrary to popular belief, I had been deemed worthy. My school believed in me before I believed in myself. They saw something that I couldn't see at the time, and that was powerful and life changing for me.

Perceptions about how we are seen by others change over time, just as our perceptions of ourselves change. We can limit ourselves to a narrow sense of who we are based on how we see ourselves, how we want to be seen or how others see us. I coach each individual to reach their highest potential, no matter what others think they are capable or not capable of. I managed to defy the odds and it wasn't easy. I never had a coach or mentor in my corner while growing up, to help me navigate my beliefs and biases. Yes, there were counsellors and psychologists, but that came with some labelling that didn't appeal to me. My role is not about fixing, because I know that, on the inside, everyone is perfect the way they are. I also know that everyone has the tools and resources within, they just need the right key to open the door. My role is to be their locksmith.

What you believe, you achieve

Studies in the field of developmental and educational psychology consistently demonstrate that a child's lack of self-belief in his/her own ability to achieve – while not lacking in actual abilities – places a handicap on their ambition, resulting in the child not reaching their life's full potential.[23] This occurs from a very young age.

The impact of negative beliefs often leads to lowered motivation, which can be interpreted by parents and educators as laziness or procrastination. If these learned behaviours are not corrected, over time the patterns become habits and the individual becomes stuck in a loop of negative thoughts.[24]

---

23 A Bandura et al, 'Self-efficacy beliefs as shapers of children's aspirations and career trajectories'

24 PR Goldin et al 'Neural mechanisms of cognitive reappraisal of negative self-beliefs in social anxiety disorder'

The teenage years are the optimal time to get to the root of negative beliefs and give young people strategies to overcome destructive habits before they become more deeply ingrained. If left unaddressed, their negative self-perception will continue into their adult lives, impacting not only their final years of high school, but their future studies, work, and emotional health and wellbeing.[25]

The reason I work with teenage girls is because I faced so much adversity and came out the other side successful. I love to help teenage girls find their unique voice. I can see things in them that they can't see in themselves, the way my high school saw things in me. I never write anyone off based on what others say, because I know there are underlying internal beliefs that each girl holds about herself. Sometimes these can't be expressed verbally and we need to look behind the behaviour to uncover the real pain in her life. It wasn't until I transitioned into high school that my internal beliefs began to shift. Starting a new school can help someone to leave the past behind and become a different person.

---

25 MR Leary and SC Atherton, 'Self-efficacy, social anxiety, and inhibition in interpersonal encounters'

I never saw myself as a leader when I was growing up. I wasn't chosen to represent the school and I didn't stand out academically or physically. After a while, though, I felt safe enough to get involved in extra-curricular activities, as long as they were group based, as I didn't want to stand out like a sore thumb. I joined the choir, ensemble and orchestra, and participated in some of the musicals (as part of the chorus, of course).

In Year 7, I was at the bottom of the intermediate classes, and possibly should have been in the lower classes, but by the time I was in Year 10, I was in advanced Maths, English, Science, Religion and Music. By Year 12, I was scoring in the top 10% of the state (NSW) in 2U Biology and 2U Music. I even received an offer to study for a Bachelor of Biomedical Sciences, specialising in human anatomy, physiology and biochemistry at the University of Wollongong. I was the first in my family to attend university, moving us from working class to middle class overnight. For someone who was told that they wouldn't amount to much, I sure did prove people wrong.

Crucially, I had made the decision *before* starting high school that I wanted to gain others' respect. I wanted respect as, in my eyes, this meant I wouldn't be bullied. I want to emphasise that this was a decision. I had made a conscious decision, a vow to myself, to focus on my mind and strengthen it academically, to help me gain the opportunities I need to thrive in this world, alongside those who were born 'normal'.

It takes daily, consistent, conscious action to turn your dreams into reality. It took six long years of striving to attain what I'd once considered unachievable. I still struggled at school to learn new concepts, because I hadn't properly learned the foundational concepts in primary school. My parents saw that I was struggling and arranged for me to have a Maths tutor in Year 8; by the end of the year, I was promoted into Advanced Maths. This proved to me, for the first time, that I *could* learn and grasp concepts, sit exams and get top marks. I wasn't stupid. After this success, my parents arranged an English tutor for me in Year 9 and, by the end of that year, I was promoted into Advanced English.

I used to believe that if you couldn't do things on your own, you were stupid. In reality, support and help were what I needed to reach the next level. I needed someone to show me a different way of learning and thinking, so I could break the negative feelings and destructive patterns inside my head. Again, this shows the importance of changing your perception and beliefs about yourself.

What doesn't kill you makes you stronger

I managed to survive Year 12 and get my arse into university. Mind you, I wouldn't want to relive the stress and pressure I placed upon myself during that final year. I didn't have the tools, strategies or people to guide and support me in the way I needed. If you're reading this book and your daughter is in her final year at high school, you may be concerned about her mental health and wellbeing during this demanding time in her life. You will know from personal experience that it isn't the be all and end all of success in life, but how can you tell her that when she's in the middle of it?

Even when I was nearing the end of high school, I was still haunted by the negative taunts kids had hurled at me during primary school. They had become little voices in my head that abused me, especially during times when I struggled or failed, when I would return to believing 'You're ugly and stupid'.

How I looked was still outside my control; there were some things I could do to improve it, but not as quickly as I would have liked. Instead, I focused all my efforts and attention on academic success. I put all my eggs in one basket, aligning my identity to academic achievement, so failure was not an option. I believed that if I didn't get into university, I would be a failure; if I didn't get in, life would continue to be marred by teasing, ridicule and disrespect. I believed that academic success would make my life perfect.

My high-school career counsellor said to me, 'If you don't get into uni, you can go to TAFE.' When I was at school, my peers, parents and I believed that TAFE (Technical and Further Education) meant you weren't smart enough for university. I devised my own plan B: if I didn't get into university I would kill myself, as punishment for my failure. Remember, I grew up with a father who promoted an all-or-nothing mindset. In his eyes, you were either a success or a failure; there was no in between. If I killed myself, at least I'd succeed at something. At the time, dying seemed more dignified than the shame and humiliation of being a 'loser'.

In truth, it was those earlier negative beliefs that were resurfacing during these times of stress and uncertainty about my future. The fear of what other people would think of me if I did not get into university; the fear of what it would mean for me. I did not really want to end my life, it was just that I couldn't see any other options. It felt like my life was all or nothing. Thankfully, I did get into university, I even got into my first choice. Would I really have killed myself if I hadn't got into university? I hope not. I know I was in a lot of pain at the time, but in truth there were other ways to navigate the uncertainties of life.

Looking back at my younger self through adult eyes, if I'd had an adult (who was not my parent or a teacher at my school) on my side, someone who was able to talk through those internal beliefs and fears with me, maybe I could have worked through my all-or-nothing approach to life. Maybe I would have been able to express my thoughts and feelings to my mentor and maybe they could have shown me that there are many paths open to us in life.

Constantly chasing the carrot at the end of the stick (ie getting into university, graduating, reaching each new milestone) never made me feel fulfilled; there was still that emptiness inside. I was either successful or not, measuring my success through the eyes of my father and societal norms. I was still chasing the holy grail of 'being normal'. But WTF is normal, anyway? I wish I'd had someone who showed me that there were other options, who didn't have any preconceived ideas about who I should or should not be.

Conclusion

It wasn't until I began working in the corporate world that I found team members coming to me for advice and mentoring. They would say, 'Geez, Paula, you'd make a great manager.' It wasn't until others started seeing leadership qualities in me that I developed an internal desire for leadership. To me, it felt like I was just doing my job, helping out fellow colleagues, but others saw leadership. Developing leadership skills gave me new tools and empowered me to be the best version of myself, to have courage and to live life with no limits.

Leadership creates a code to live by, because it puts you in the driver's seat; everyone is looking to you for guidance, it helps you to step up. Leadership requires an understanding of yourself – you can't lead others unless you can lead yourself. Thankfully, by the time this happened, I'd already developed an internal sense of my identity. I knew who I was and was able to lead myself. Yet I still needed someone else to release this potential by seeing it in me. Like Captain Marvel, I'd finally identified who I was and now I could fly. I went from being invisible to visible; from feeling like a victim to a victor; from feeling like my life was controlled by others to feeling in control of myself.

I became a Limited Edition Leader. The leading lady of my own destiny, the best gift I could ever give myself. As parents, we want to raise daughters who are the best possible versions of themselves, better than we were at their age. We don't want to spend our lives worrying about all the little choices our daughter makes along the path of life, the types of people that might enter into it and influence her decisions. If we give her the tools and insights now, she can develop her own leadership mindset. Then, when unforeseen influences present themselves, as they will, she will have the skills and capabilities to deal with them.

A goal without a plan is just a wish

I'd like to take the opportunity to challenge you on what's next in your life plan. How will you create confidence and conquer life? The Covid-19 pandemic forced us all to live outside our comfort zones. The challenge now is to maintain our growth mindset, motivation and momentum during this period of uncertainty. How can we minimise the stress of disruptions? What are your goals for the next two to six months? Do you have a game plan or have you thrown it out the window? Are you sitting back, watching and waiting to see what happens next?

What if we were proactive instead of reactive? What if, instead of waiting to find out when it will be business as usual, let's get our teens moving forward as quickly and in the most stress-free way possible. Let's empower them to move ahead of the game, while others are still watching and waiting.

Set your daughter on the right track with the mindset, motivation and momentum to reach her life goals. Then she'll be well ahead of the curve. A leadership mindset is all about being ahead of the general curve; about knowing what moves to make and how to mitigate in advance; about having confidence, courage and certainty in one's self and abilities.

Below are five topics you can begin to work through right now with your daughter:

1. **What:** What is it that she wants to achieve? Always start with the end in mind.

2. **Why:** What is her purpose, her life mission? What makes her face light up when she talks about it? What subjects does she enjoy without external motivation?

3. **How:** How is she going to achieve her goals? How will she know that she is successful? What does success look and feel like for her? What is her measurement of success?

4. **When:** What is the deadline to achieve each goal?

5. **Who:** Successful people never do things alone; they have a team of specialists or supporters to help them navigate their journey, to assist them to reach their final destination, successfully and on time. Ideally, every girl will have five

people focused on the five aspects of her wellbeing:

- Mental

- Financial

- Emotional

- Spiritual

- Physical

The ancient Greek stoic philosopher Epictetus, in the book *The Enchiridion*, is quoted as saying, 'One of the best ways to elevate your character immediately is to find worthy role models to emulate.'[26] Having five such people is an ideal, and it may not be feasible in reality. What is important is that there is more than just parents trying to do it all. When you are working through these steps with your daughter, remember that the key is consistency, but don't be afraid to reassess goals and tweak as needed.

Successful athletes never go it alone; they always have a coach to help show them the way. These coaches have prior knowledge and experience that they draw on to offer advice

---

26 Epictetus, *The Enchiridion*

and encouragement. They have travelled the path before and can explain what to look for and avoid and suggest options to try along the journey. An athlete would never compete without a coach; it would be just as disadvantageous for someone to go it alone in the game of life when there are valuable coaches, guides and mentors available.

A worthy guide can take us to the edge of our comfort zone, shepherd us through the fear zone and safely into the thrill of growth and development. They show us the way, tell us what tools and skills we'll need, and advise us when to jump and when to hold back. Having a coach is a positive experience. Coaches don't fix you, they simply enable and enhance what you already have within.

I've channelled my experience and expertise into one-on-one coaching and group leadership programmes, workshops, seminars and keynote speeches for teenage girls and young women. I've created a foundation of leadership skills that embed the belief 'you are enough' into their identities, creating new strategies for girls to live their best lives. I am excited to help the next generation of women to create the confidence to conquer life, their way.

I used to wish I was normal, so I could fit in, be liked and loved. Eventually, I realised that if that had happened, I may have lost sight of who I am and who I was destined to be in this world. Why would I strive to fit in, when I was clearly born to stand out? This is a hard lesson to learn and is something that I work on with young girls and women. The teenage years are tough. We've all been there and now we're watching history repeat itself. It takes a village to raise a child, sometimes people need help to embrace their uniqueness. My motto is: 'It's not how you start in life that counts, it's how you choose to live it.'

So, go out there, be you, have the courage to be confident and conquer life.

References

Archard, N, 'Adolescent girls and leadership: The impact of confidence, competition, and failure', *International Journal of Adolescence and Youth*, 17/2 (2012), https://doi.org/10.1080/02673843.2011.649431

Archard, N, 'Women's participation as leaders in society: An adolescent girls' perspective', *Journal of Youth Studies*, 16/6 (2013), pp759–775, https://doi.org/10.1080/13676261.2012.756974

Bandura, A, Barbaranelli, C, Caprara, GV and Pastorelli, C, 'Self-efficacy beliefs as shapers of children's aspirations and career trajectories', *Child Development,*

72 (2001), pp187–206, https://doi.
org/10.1111/1467-8624.00273

De Luca, L, Nocentini, A and Menesini, E,
'The teacher's role in preventing bullying',
Frontiers in Psychology, 10 (2019), pp1–9,
https://doi.org/10.3389/fpsyg.2019.01830

Eckman, P, *Emotions Revealed: Recognizing
faces and feelings to improve communication and
emotional life* (St. Martin's Press, 2007)

Epictetus, *The Enchiridion*, (12th Media
Services, 2018)

Goldin, PR, Manber-Ball, T, Werner,
K, Heimberg, R and Gross, JJ, 'Neural
mechanisms of cognitive reappraisal
of negative self-beliefs in social anxiety
disorder', *Biological Psychiatry*, 66 (2009),
pp1091–1099, https://doi.org/10.1016/j.
biopsych.2009.07.014

Hopwood, A, 'Jung's model of the Psyche'
(The Society of Analytical Psychology,
no date), www.thesap.org.uk/resources/
articles-on-jungian-psychology-2/
carl-gustav-jung/jungs-model-psyche

Hügelschäfer, S and Achtziger, A, 'On confident men and rational women: It's all on your mind(set)', *Journal of Economic Psychology* (2013), pp1–12, https://doi.org/10.1016/j.joep.2013.04.001

Isaacs, E, 'Women and leadership report', *Business Chicks* (2018), https://businesschicks.com/wp-content/uploads/2018/11/CLA_Movers-and-Breakers-Influence-with-Impact-Summary1.pdf

Jellinger, KA, 'Funktionelle Pathophysiologie des Bewusstseins [Functional pathophysiology of consciousness]', *Neuropsychiatry*, 23/2 (2009), pp115–33, https://pubmed.ncbi.nlm.nih.gov/19573504

Kay, K and Shipman, C, *The Confidence Code: The science and art of self-assurance – what women should know* (HarperCollins, 2014)

Leary, MR and Atherton, SC, 'Self-efficacy, social anxiety, and inhibition in interpersonal encounters', *Journal of Social and Clinical Psychology*, 4 (1986), pp256–267, https://doi.org/10.1521/jscp.1986.4.3.256

Müller-Pinzler, L, Czekalla, N, Mayer, AV et al, 'Negativity bias in forming beliefs about own abilities', *Scientific Reports*, 9/14416 (2019), https://doi.org/10.1038/s41598-019-50821-w

Müller-Pinzler, L, Gazzola, V, Keysers, C et al, 'Neural pathways of embarrassment and their modulation by social anxiety', *NeuroImage*, 119 (2015), pp252–261, https://doi.org/10.1016/j.neuroimage.2015.06.036

Newman, BM and Newman, PR, *Theories of Adolescent Development* (Academic Press Elsevier, 2020)

Ng, B, 'The neuroscience of growth mindset and intrinsic motivation', *Brain Sciences*, 26/1 (2018), https://doi.org/10.3390/brainsci8020020

Sinek, S, *Start with Why: How great leaders inspire everyone to take action* (Portfolio, 2009)

Steinmetz, J et al, 'Being observed magnifies action', *Journal of Personality and Social Psychology*, 111 (2016), pp852–865, https://doi.org/10.1037/pspi0000065

Stoycheva, M and Ruskov, P, 'Growth mindset development pattern', *Proceedings of the 20th European Conference on Pattern Languages of Programs*, 7 (2015) https://doi.org/10.1145/2855321.2855329

Thoreau, HD, *Walden* (Penguin, 2016)

Team Tony, 'How to get what you deserve: Transform your mindset and achieve your dreams in eight steps' (TonyRobbins.com, no date), www.tonyrobbins.com/mind-meaning/get-what-you-deserve

Vaillancourt, T, 'Do human females use indirect aggression as an intrasexual competition strategy?', *Philosophical Transactions of the Royal Society B*, 368 (2013), pp1–7, https://doi.org/10.1098/rstb.2013.0080

Yeo, SS, Chang, PH and Jang, SH, 'The ascending reticular activating system from pontine reticular formation to the thalamus in the human brain', *Frontiers in Human Neuroscience*, 7 (2013), p416, https://doi.org/10.3389/fnhum.2013.00416

Further Reading

Archard, N, 'Developing future women leaders: The importance of mentoring and role modeling in the girls' school context', *Mentoring and Tutoring: Partnership in Learning*, 20/4 (2012), pp451–472, https://doi.org/10.1080/13611267.2012.725980

Archard, N, 'Female Leadership Framework: Developing adolescent girls as future women leaders through the formation of a female leadership identity', *Leading and Managing*, 19/1 (2013), pp51–71, https://researchers.mq.edu.au/en/publications/female-leadership-framework-developing-adolescent-girls-as-future

Archard, N, 'Preparing adolescent girls for school and post-school leadership: recommendations to school educators from educational staff, female students, and women leaders', *International Journal of Adolescence and Youth*, 16/7 (2012), pp1–18, https://doi.org/10.1080/02673843.2012.666799

Archard, N, 'Women's participation as leadership in society: an adolescent girls' perspective', *Journal of Youth Studies'*, 16/7 (2013), pp1–17, https://doi.org/10.1080/13676261.2012.756974

Brown, B, *Daring Greatly: How the courage to be vulnerable transforms the way we live, love, parent and lead* (Penguin Random House, 2012)

Brown, B, *The Gifts of Imperfection: Let go of who you think you're supposed to be and embrace who you are* (Hazelden, 2010)

Capacchione, L, *Recovery of Your Inner Child: The highly acclaimed method for liberating your inner self* (Simon & Schuster, 1991)

Cheal, C, 'The Role of Moods in NLP', *Acuity*, 1/1 (2010), pp28–36, www.gwiznlp.com/

wp-content/uploads/2014/08/The-Role-of-Moods-in-NLP.pdf

Cooper, D, *Smart Parenting: How to develop your child's mindset, resilience and courage for the future of work* (Hoogi, 2018)

Dweck, CS, *Mindset: The new psychology of success* (Ballantine Books, 2016)

Faber, A and Mazlish, E, *How to Talk so Teens Will Listen and Listen so Teens Will Talk* (Piccadilly, 2006)

Ferguson, K and Fox, C, *Women Kind: Unlocking the power of women supporting women* (Murdoch Books, 2018)

Grinder, M, 'School: A Private Club for Visuals: Expanding the membership by using non-verbal visuals' (2005), pp1–31, www.michaelgrinder.com

Grinder, M, *Surviving your Teen's Adolescence* (2019), https://michaelgrinder.com/product/ebook-surviving-your-teens-adolescence

Neuharth, D, *If You Had Controlling Parents: How to make peace with your past and take your place in the world* (Harper Collins, 1998)

Neuharth, D, *Secrets You Keep From Yourself: How to stop sabotaging your happiness* (St Martin's Press, 2004)

Rosenberg, M, *The Chameleon: Life-changing wisdom for anyone who has a personality or knows someone who does* (Take Flight Learning, 2016)

Selby, E, Anestis, M and Joiner, T, 'Understanding the relationship between emotional and behavioral dysregulation: Emotional cascades', *Behaviour Research and Therapy*, 46 (2008), pp593–611, https://doi.org/10.1016/j.brat.2008.02.002

Seligman, M, *Learned Optimism: How to change your mind and your life* (Random House, 1992)

Siderovski, J, *Empowering Your Soul: Legacy of her mind* (Lulu Publishing, 2016)

Spicer, T, *The Good Girl Stripped Bare* (Harper Collins, 2017)

Trimm, C, *The 40 Day Soul Fast: Your journey to authentic living* (Destiny Image, 2011)

Wilding, C, *How to Deal with Low Self-Esteem: A 5-step, CBT-based plan for overcoming negative thoughts and eliminating self-doubt* (Hodder & Stoughton, 2015)

Acknowledgements

First, I would like to thank my parents, Katherine and Victor, who have since passed from this Earth, who raised me to be the woman I am today. They may not have always got it right, but their input gave me insights and the ability to understand other people's views of the world. I also learned from them how others' views can impact your life long term if you let them control your destiny.

To my husband, Paul, for being my male champion and cheering me on, especially during the tough times.

To my Leadership Advisory Board (both past and present): Professor Gary Martin,

Julie Hyam-Elliot, Reverend David Smith, Jodi Sampson, Merrick Rosenberg and The Honourable Victor Perton.

Thank you for believing in me and understanding the impact I wanted to make in the world through my business before it even got off the ground, and for your mentorship, guidance, support and friendship over the years. You have kept me centred, focused and on track to my true north, especially during times of setback. For this I am enormously grateful.

Lastly, I want to thank my editor, Alison Fraser. Without her support, this book would not have reached the final stage of publication.

There are so many people who have been part of my business journey who I haven't been able to cover here, but to all of you, I thank you from the bottom of my heart.

The Author

**It's not how you start off in life that counts;
it's how you choose to live it.**

Paula Dunn is a teenage resilience expert and cognitive scientist who works with teenagers, parents and educators to position them for maximum impact in their studies, personal and professional lives. Paula believes that developing strong identities provides the building blocks for living as your authentic self.

Paula has over twenty years' experience delivering award-winning people leadership strategies for iconic and international brands such as Eli Lily, Johnson & Johnson, and Cochlear.

With qualifications including Bachelor of Biomedical Sciences (Hons), Master of Science (Hons), Master Practitioner in Business Coaching and Executive Leadership, a Diploma and Advanced Diploma in Life Coaching, and Master Practitioner of NLP, Paula is also an accredited speaker, coach, facilitator and trainer.

She was the 2018 Regional Finalist in the category Superstar Start Up Awards, the 2019 Inner West Regional Finalist for Local Business Awards and was awarded the prestigious Women of Excellence award for her leadership programme for Year 10 girls at the Women Economic Forum in India 2019. Paula was a finalist in two categories at the Illawarra Women in Business Awards 2020, the Business Woman of the Year and Small Business of the Year categories, and a 2020 finalist in the Illawarra Business Chamber's 'Inspiring Business Leader' award.

For her ongoing work with teens, Paula was also named among the Top 50 Global Key

Influencers in the prestigious humanitarian magazine, *eYs Magazine*.

Paula has worked one-on-one with hundreds of clients in high schools, academia and the corporate world and is a sought-after media commentator on leadership and resilience.

Contact

🌐 www.nolimitsconsulting.com.au

🌐 www.pauladunn.com.au

in www.linkedin.com/in/pauladunn